The BENJAMIN FRANKLIN
You Never Knew

BY JAMES LINCOLN COLLIER

Children's Press®
A Division of Scholastic Inc.
New York Toronto London Auckland Sydney
Mexico City New Delhi Hong Kong
Danbury, Connecticut

Library of Congress Cataloging-in-Publication Data

Collier, James Lincoln, 1928-
The Benjamin Franklin you never knew / James Lincoln Collier.
    p. cm.
  Includes bibliographical references and index.
  ISBN 0-516-24427-2
  1. Franklin, Benjamin, 1706-1790—Juvenile literature. 2. Statesmen—United
States—Biography—Juvenile literature. 3. Scientists—United States—Biogra-
phy—Juvenile literature. 4. Printers—United States—Biography—Juvenile lit-
erature. 5. Inventors—United States—Biography—Juvenile literature. I. Title.
  E302.6.F8C68 2004
  973.3'092—dc22

                        2003028194

Illustrations by Greg Copeland
Book design by A. Natacha Pimentel C.

Photographs © 2004: American Philosophical Society: 4, 7, 9, 13, 25, 57; Art
Resource, NY: 46 (Erich Lessing), 74 (Private Collection), 67 (Reunion des
Musees Nationaux); Bridgeman Art Library International Ltd., London/New
York: 65 (Delaware Art Museum, Wilmington, USA, Howard Pyle Collection),
41 (Library Company of Philadelphia, PA, USA), 61, 69 (Library of Congress,
Washington D.C., USA), 71 (The Detroit Institute of Arts, USA, Gift of Dexter
M. Ferry Jr.); Corbis Images: cover, back cover, 36, 52 (Bettmann), 62; Mary
Evans Picture Library: 22, 39, 43, 45; North Wind Picture Archives: 1, 17, 18, 24,
27, 30, 32, 33, 49, 50.

CONTENTS

Chapter 1

A SELF-IMPROVING BOY

BENJAMIN FRANKLIN WAS THE FIRST famous American. Of course, others had been known about. Americans knew about the early Pilgrim fathers like Miles Standish and William Brewster. Peter Stuyvesant, a Dutchman who was governor of New Amsterdam (now New York City), was a renowned character. And during Franklin's lifetime, George Washington would become the most famous American of all, as he perhaps still is.

Probably the most famous picture of Ben Franklin, this shows him studying a paper or report at the time he was living in England.

But Benjamin Franklin was the first American who was celebrated in both America and Europe. His portrait was painted again and again. Statues were made of him. Poems were written about him. Great men, even kings, wanted to meet him.

Why? What had he done that was so important? For one thing, he "tamed the lightning." We shall hear more about that in a little while.

For another thing, he was considered a wise man, a great philosopher with much knowledge of science, the arts, and literature. In Franklin's time, and for many years after, Europeans considered Americans to be rough frontiersmen and women who could barely read and write. Americans, most Europeans thought, had no understanding of the high culture of art, literature, and music that had developed in Europe over many centuries. Americans knew nothing but how to hunt bears, chop wood, and grow corn. They did not have the manners and refinement of European ladies and gentlemen. So, when Ben Franklin came along—a writer, inventor, philosopher, scientist, and statesman—Europeans were astounded. They had not believed that America could produce such a person.

And, indeed, Europeans were right about one thing, Benjamin Franklin was a remarkable person.

But Europeans then, and a great many people today, do not really understand why we celebrate Franklin. True, he tamed lightning. True, he wrote some books that are interesting to read more than 250 years later. But what really makes Ben Franklin important is the role he played in helping what came to be called the United States become a great and independent nation. Benjamin Franklin did not build the United States all by himself, tens of thousands of Americans did that. But the part he played was critically important. He was the right man in the right place at the right time.

Ben's father, Josiah, had come to America from England in 1683, when the country was still very new. He settled in Boston, which was at the moment perhaps the most important city in North America. It was, however, really a country town of a few thousand people. Boston was made up mainly of one- and two-story houses and shops. The streets were made of dirt that swirled with dust in the summer and sloshed with mud in wet weather. There was a big "common," or green, in the middle of the town, where people grazed their milk cows. Ships came and went in the bustling harbor. Much of the wealth of the city came from fishermen, who caught countless tons of the codfish that swarmed in the nearby Atlantic. Salted down, the fish would keep for weeks, and were sold in Europe and the Caribbean, as well as to the other British colonies. Bigger ships carried the produce of the fields and forests, such as wheat, cornmeal, deerskins, beaver fur, and timber, from Boston to ports everywhere.

Benjamin's father had seven children by his first wife, who died, and ten more by his second wife. Ben, born in January 1706, was the fifteenth child.

His father worked first as a dyer and then as a candle maker, selling his goods from a small shop. With a large family to support, Josiah was endlessly busy at his trade of candle making. Everybody in the family had to help, including Ben, who found the work very boring.

Nonetheless, Josiah Franklin did what he could to raise his children properly. We must remember that in those days, when people did not have a lot of toys, a television or video games for amusement, they took more interest in serious matters, like religion and politics. Josiah Franklin liked to ask friends to dinner to talk about such subjects for the benefit of his children. Benjamin Franklin grew up hearing many conversations on the important topics of the day such as new opinions on religion and how best to deal with America's rulers in England.

We have two stories about young Ben Franklin that tell us something about the kind of boy he was. As in most families of that time, his father always said a long prayer before each meal, thanking God for the food on the table, while the hungry children sat with bowed heads waiting to eat. Once, young Benjamin was helping his father salt down a barrel of meat for the coming

An engraving of the house in which Franklin was born—not very large for a family with so many children.

winter. He said, "I think, Father, if you were to say grace over the whole cask—once and for all—it would be a vast saving of time." Even as a boy, Ben was very practical, always looking for new and ingenious ways of saving time and doing things better.

The second story has to do with Ben's efforts to learn to swim. In those days modern swimming methods had not been worked out. Many people did not know how to swim. Ben, who always wanted to improve himself, decided he must learn to swim. He set about it very methodically. For instance, he would walk into the water up to his chest, face toward the shore, and throw an egg in the direction of the beach. "It will sink to the bottom," he later explained, "and be easily seen there, as your water is clear." He would then swim underwater to it, pick it up, and repeat the process, each time forcing himself to swim down to the egg.

He also invented small paddles that he would hold in his hand or strap to his feet to give him extra swimming power. "I swam faster by means of these pallets, but they fatigued my wrists." The ones he attached to his feet had drawbacks as well. "I observed that the stroke is partly given by the insides of the feet and the ankles, and not entirely with the soles of the feet." Here are three sides to Franklin's personality that would be immensely important to his success: his determination to improve himself, his inventiveness, and his habit of carefully analyzing the things he was involved with.

One aspect of his concern for self-improvement was his interest in books. At that time books were scarce and expensive. There were few newspapers and no magazines. Franklin borrowed whatever books he could, from whomever he could, and read constantly. Sometimes he would sit up most of the night reading in order to finish a book before it had to be returned.

He read many religious books, as people did at the time, as well as history and poetry. Out of this boyhood habit grew a great love of books and reading that would last him all his life. He came to understand that while there are many things that can't be learned from books, there are many that can't be learned anywhere else, such as what went on in the past, or what is going on in foreign lands.

Ben was sent to school for only two years, when he was eight to ten years old. Despite this, he jumped ahead very quickly, not only of children of his own age but of many adults, too.

But young Ben could not spend his life swimming and reading. Like everybody else, he had to work. In those days many town boys were sent out as apprentices to learn a trade. They would work for nothing for several years—often seven—for a shoemaker, silversmith, leather worker, or butcher. This way they would learn a business, and in time start their own little shop, perhaps with apprentices of their own.

Ben's father considered various trades for him. As it happened, Ben had an older half-brother who was a printer. As Ben was such a good reader, it made sense to apprentice him to a printer, where his ability to spell and punctuate would be of use. So at age twelve, Ben went to work for his half-brother James.

The printing trade was of course much different from what it is today, with our high-speed presses and computer-set type. In Ben's time each letter was on a small, separate piece of metal. They were held in a case—all the *e's* in one compartment, all the *c's* in another, and so forth. A typesetter rapidly "set" the letters in a frame that represented a page. The letters had to be set backward, from right to left, so that they would come out left to right when printed. The frame was placed in the press and inked. A lever pulled the type down onto a sheet of paper lying on the press bed. The process was repeated until the required number of pages was printed.

Franklin at work as a printer. Note the simple flatbed press. By turning a wheel, Franklin could press the inked type against each sheet of paper, one letter at a time.

Such a system would be far too slow for modern newspapers with "print runs" of hundreds of thousands of copies a day, each fifty or a hundred pages long. But it worked for books and newspapers of the time, which often had runs of only a few thousand—or even a few hundred—copies.

Ben quickly became a good printer, able to set type rapidly and space out the lines to make them even. He learned what types of paper were best for certain jobs, how to make ink, the different kinds of types to be used for books and advertisements. James's shop printed all sorts of things, like forms for bills, advertisement posters, even patterns on cloth.

In 1721 James Franklin decided to start a newspaper, which he called the *New England Courant*. Newspapers were a relatively new invention. They were small, made up of only a few pages. They had only a few simple advertisements. Sometimes people paid the printer to run stories and articles they wanted published. Such newspapers carried jokes, poems, and stories as well as the usual political articles.

For Ben the job at the *New England Courant* was an education. It brought a lot of writers and politicians into the printing shop with their stories and articles. Ben eagerly listened to them talk about writing style and the political and social activities they wrote about.

As a boy who wanted to improve himself, Ben soon decided to write something, too. He was only fifteen, however, and he knew that James would not allow a mere boy to write for his newspaper. So Ben wrote a short satirical piece, supposedly by a widow he named Silence Dogood. He did not sign it, but at night slipped it under the door to the print shop. In the morning James found the piece. He read it and passed it around to others there. Everybody began saying how good the piece was. Ben did not tell them he had written it, but listened to the others try to guess who might have written it, naming "men of some character among us for learning and ingenuity."

James quickly published the Silence Dogood piece in his newspaper. Over the next few months Ben wrote more Dogood articles. He still did not tell anyone he was the author, for the pieces were comical and some-what impolite, and he was afraid his brother would be angry with him. Eventually these pieces were collected and published in a book called the *Dogood Papers*. The book was quite successful. Ben Franklin never told anyone he had written it. He had been dead for many years before anyone discovered the truth.

At sixteen, Ben Franklin was getting ahead. He was, however, a very independent-minded boy. He disliked being ordered around by his older brother, as younger brothers often do. Sometimes Ben talked back to James and would get hit. Eventually Ben decided he had had enough. He wanted to be on his own.

But, he was supposed to serve out his apprenticeship to James. He would have to run away to another city. So, very quietly, he sold a few of his books to get boat fare and slipped away to New York.

When he got there, he sought out a printer and asked him for a job. The printer did not need a helper, but said that his son, who was a printer in Philadelphia, did. Ben then made his way to Philadelphia. His money had just about run out. He arrived tired and hungry with a handful of change. He spent his change on three huge rolls and strolled into his new hometown carrying one roll under each arm and eating the third one. In this fashion he started his rise to fame.

This picture shows Franklin carrying cases of type along the streets of Philadelphia. A printing shop had many different sizes and styles of type.

Chapter 2

THE RISING STAR

IT SHOULD BE CLEAR THAT AT THE AGE OF seventeen, Ben Franklin was a boy—a young man, really—who was determined to make a success of himself. In 1723 Philadelphia was a good place to do it, for it was rapidly catching up to Boston as America's most important city. The rich farms of the surrounding countryside produced large quantities of grain, meat, and other products that could be bought and sold by Philadelphia merchants. There were steel, paper, and other types of mills in the city. Some of the citizens were growing wealthy and building themselves fine houses.

A picture of Franklin at about age twenty, when he was beginning to make a name for himself as a printer in Philadelphia.

For Benjamin Franklin it was a land of opportunity. He found his way to the shop owned by the son of the New York printer. The son had already found a new helper, so he sent Ben over to the other printer in town. There he was promptly hired. As it happened, the printers in Philadelphia were not very experienced. Franklin saw that he was a much better printer than they were. He was soon taking charge of much of the work in the shop. Very quickly he made a reputation as a printer. He even made an extended trip to England to study printing methods, advancing his skills even more. People began to notice him. In 1727 one of the other workers in his shop said that if Franklin would go into partnership with him in their own printing shop, the man's father would lend them the money for it. Franklin agreed.

Now Franklin had his own print shop and was ready to push ahead. He realized that it was important to impress other people. He made a point of being "industrious and frugal," as he said. "I never went out a-fishing or shooting . . . and, to show that I was not above my business, I sometimes brought home the paper I purchased at the stores through the streets on a wheelbarrow." Franklin believed that it was not enough to work hard and not be too proud. You had to make sure other people realized it. He was not trying to fool anybody, but he wanted to make sure he got credit for the things he did.

He knew, further, that he could not get wealthy simply by running a printing shop. He understood the newspaper business, and he decided he wanted a paper of his own. He of course wanted to make money from his newspaper, but he also knew that anyone who ran a newspaper could become very influential if the paper was well liked and widely read.

Franklin's shop in Philadelphia. It is still visited every year by many tourists.

There was at the time only one newspaper in Philadelphia and not more than a handful scattered around the American colonies. As it worked out, Franklin was able to buy the Philadelphia newspaper in 1729. He renamed it the *Pennsylvania Gazette*. Franklin wrote much of the newspaper himself, but he had gotten to know some very good writers, and they also contributed articles. Franklin saw to it that the *Pennsylvania Gazette* carried not only the latest news, but also interesting political articles, funny stories, and jokes. Soon it was considered the best newspaper in the area, one of the best in the American colonies.

Next Franklin started to publish books, among them a medical book and a famous English novel called *Pamela*. It was one of the first novels to be published in the American colonies. Then he started a magazine called the *General Magazine and Historical*

Chronicle for All the British Plantations in America (long titles were fashionable in those days). It contained the first magazine advertisement ever printed in what would become the United States. The ad was for a ferry across the Potomac River.

Finally, in 1732 he started his most famous publication, *Poor Richard's Almanac*. Franklin wrote it under the pseudonym (pen name) Richard Saunders. Almanacs were popular in those days. They contained a lot of information that people needed. Farmers wanted to know the times of sunrises and sunsets, when the moon would wax and wane, whether to expect a hard or an easy winter. Fishermen needed to know the times of the high and low tides. Everybody wanted to know when to expect eclipses and other celestial events.

Most almanacs spiced up these rather dry tables of tides and sunrises with jokes, little stories, folk sayings, and whatever else the editor could think of. Franklin was very clever at making up stories and working out his own sayings. He did not of course make up all the aphorisms, or sayings, that appeared in *Poor Richard's Almanac*, but he made up many of them. Some that he printed were, "He that riseth late must trot all day" and "He's a fool that makes his doctor his heir."

Poor Richard's Almanac was a great success and made Benjamin Franklin a lot of money. By this time Franklin had bought out his partner in the business. He had a shop where he sold not only the books that he printed, but other books as well. He sold all kinds of official forms, a special type of soap that his family in Boston made, cheese, tea, coffee, goose feathers for pillows, and much else. Benjamin Franklin was not ashamed to make an honest dollar any way that he could.

But it had to be an honest dollar. One day a man came into his shop with an article he wanted Franklin to publish in the *Pennsylvania Gazette*. He offered to pay Franklin some money to print it, as was often done at the time.

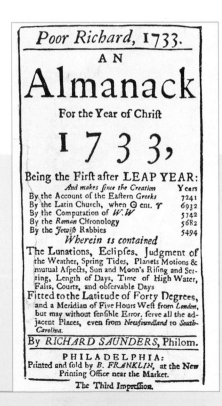

Poor Richard, 1733.
AN
Almanack
For the Year of Christ
1733,
Being the First after LEAP YEAR:

And makes since the Creation Years
By the Account of the Eastern Greeks 7241
By the Latin Church, when ☉ ent. ♈ 6932
By the Computation of *W. W* 5742
By the *Roman* Chronology 5682
By the *Jewish* Rabbies 5494

Wherein is contained

The Lunations, Eclipses, Judgment of the Weather, Spring Tides, Planets Motions & mutual Aspects, Sun and Moon's Rising and Setting, Length of Days, Time of High Water, Fairs, Courts, and observable Days

Fitted to the Latitude of Forty Degrees, and a Meridian of Five Hours West from *London*, but may without sensible Error, serve all the adjacent Places, even from *Newfoundland* to *South-Carolina*.

By *RICHARD SAUNDERS*, Philom.

PHILADELPHIA:
Printed and sold by B. FRANKLIN, at the New Printing Office near the Market.

The Third Impression.

The title page of Poor Richard's Almanac. *(At the time, s was written much like a modern f.) Almanacs like this contained a jumble of information, some of it useful—like the times of high and low tides. Franklin filled his almanac with little sayings and brief stories of unusual events.*

Franklin took the article home to read. He found it rude and insulting. The next morning he told the man that he had eaten nothing but a loaf of bread for his supper, had slept on the floor wrapped in his overcoat, and had had only bread and water for breakfast. He said that so long as he could stand to live on bread and water and sleep on the floor he did not have to take anybody's money to print something he didn't think should be printed.

So he prospered, and in time felt he had enough money to start a family. In 1730 he married Deborah Read. He had a son, William, and then a second son, Francis, whom he called young Franky. Sadly, when he was only four, Franky died of smallpox, a common and deadly disease of the time. Ben was bitterly unhappy at the death of his little boy.

Franklin's wife, Deborah Read. Franklin spent much of his life living in foreign places, leaving her to manage things by herself at home. She often longed for him to return to her.

When he moved to London thirty years later he brought with him a little portrait of Franky, whom he thought of often. He wrote that the boy was seldom "equaled in everything, and whom to this day I cannot think of without a sigh." In 1743 Franklin had another child, this one a girl named Sarah, whom they always called Sally.

By this time Franklin was prospering in business and becoming well known in Philadelphia. But he was always ambitious to rise up to the next step. And the next step was to go into politics.

In the mid-1700s the political situation was complicated. We need to understand it to see the importance of what Benjamin Franklin would eventually do for his nation. As students of American history know, by the 1730s, when Ben was publishing his newspaper and starting his family, what would become the United States consisted of thirteen colonies, running from New Hampshire in the north to Georgia in the south. All of them belonged to England, but they had been established piecemeal, and each had a somewhat different relationship with the mother country. They were like thirteen little boats being tugged along by a grand ship.

There was no overall government in the colonies. Each one had a governor appointed by the English king (or his officials) and an assembly of Americans mainly elected by the voters of that colony. Inevitably there was a great deal of noisy quarreling over power. The colonists insisted they ought to have more say in how their colony was run. This was especially so in the case of taxes. The colonists most certainly did not like the English government telling them how much tax they must pay.

During the 1760s and beyond, Americans were growing increasingly troubled by British control of their affairs. People frequently met to discuss the problem, as in this picture. Tempers were often high.

The English government, on the other hand, believed that it ought to have the final say on everything, including taxes. In the end there would be a show-down—the American Revolution.

This was all complicated enough, but there were a lot of other actors in the play. Spain held land in what is now Florida, as well as a great deal more in the far west. The French held Canada and New Orleans, giving them control of both ends of the Mississippi River. They were also trying to gain control of what was then called the Northwest Territory. This was the land north of the Ohio River, between the Allegheny Mountains and the Mississippi. It was very fertile land, mostly covered with forest, and filled with game such as deer, beaver, bear, and even buffalo. Everybody realized that this Northwest Territory was very valuable.

The English colonists, however, were growing short of land in their area between the Atlantic Ocean and the Allegheny Mountains. This was partly because immigrants, who needed farmland, were flooding in. And partly it was because the land was getting worn out, and the trees necessary for firewood, furniture, and home building were mostly gone. American colonists were therefore slipping over the Allegheny Mountains into the Northwest Territory, where they cut down trees to make farms. Their English rulers in London were eager for the colonists to stake out land in the Northwest Territory so it would fall into English, rather than French, hands.

So the English and the French were competing for control of the Northwest Territory. Moreover, during this period they were often fighting each other in Europe as well. They were, in fact, ancient rivals.

But there was a third party involved in the Northwest Territory. This party was made up of several tribes of Indians who happened to live there. Some of these Indian tribes had been trading with the English and their settlers for many years, mainly swapping furs for goods like metal pots, metal axes, knives, swords, and of course guns and gunpowder. However, the majority of the Indians had been dealing with the French. They tended to favor the French, especially as it was the English colonists who were cutting down their forests and scaring off the game they needed for food. The French, of course, were perfectly happy to see the Indians fighting off the English settlers. They were glad to supply them with guns and gunpowder. On the English side, the colonists were enraged with the French for giving weapons to the Indians, who might use them to kill English settlers.

Unlike the English, the French were less interested in settling the new country than in taking natural products from it. They traded with the Indians, especially for furs. Here, some French traders camp by the bank of a river.

There were a lot of people quarreling with each other—the English against the French, the colonists against their rulers in London, the Indians against anyone who was trying to take over their lands. Franklin would plunge into this political whirlpool. He would spend most of the rest of his life trying to calm the waters. In so doing, he would help to create the United States of America.

His first important political job was as clerk to the Pennsylvania Assembly, the group of people that made the laws. He was appointed in 1736. This job was routine, but it put him in touch with important politicians. The next year he was also appointed deputy postmaster for Philadelphia. (People were allowed to hold two jobs of this kind at once.) Not surprisingly, he quickly saw ways to improve the mail service.

Franklin next, almost by himself, created a militia for the colony. A militia was something like our national guard—companies of men in towns and villages who drilled once a week and stayed alert in order to leap to the defense of the colony if necessary.

Pennsylvania was under threat from the French, who boldly sailed into the Delaware River almost to Philadelphia. The colony's settlers across the Alleghenies were also worried about Indian attacks. Franklin wrote a piece for his newspaper and a pamphlet called *Plain Truth*, urging his fellow citizens to form a militia. He called a meeting at which he made a speech, and before long some ten thousand men had signed up and organized themselves into militia companies.

This accomplishment showed Pennsylvanians that Franklin was not just a printer and newspaper editor, but also a man who could get things done. It also annoyed the British authorities. One said that Franklin was "a dangerous man, and I should be glad if he inhabited any other country, as I believe him of a very uneasy spirit. However, as he is a sort of tribune of the people, he must be treated with regard." By this he meant that the citizens of Pennsylvania were beginning to look to Franklin for advice on how to protect themselves from the British government.

Franklin's star was rising. A few years later he was elected to the Assembly, and he immediately became one of the most influential people in it. In 1753 he was one of three men on a committee to make a treaty of

In the American colonies men organized themselves into militia companies for defense against their enemies—the French, the Indians, and eventually the British. Usually these militia elected their own officers. Inexperienced militias were sometimes the subject of jokes, as in this caricature. In fact many militia companies fought well.

friendship with some local Indians. The same year, he was appointed by the British government to the post of head of the mails for all thirteen colonies. The British may have considered him dangerous, but they also knew that he would do an excellent job. And he did. He immediately set off on a three-thousand-mile trip around the colonies to see how he could improve the postal system.

By this time the conflict in the Northwest Territory was growing worse. The French had begun to build a line of forts there. With these forts and the help of the Indians, they hoped to fence the English colonists out of the area. To stop them, the British government asked the colonies that bordered on the Northwest Territory to join together to fight off the French. In this way, the British hoped, the colonists would be forced to pay for a lot of the costs of their own defense. A conference was set for June 1754 at Albany, New York, to work out a plan.

Inevitably, Ben Franklin was chosen as one of the delegates from Pennsylvania to go to this conference. Always thinking ahead, Franklin immediately sat down and worked out a scheme for uniting the colonies involved. At the same time, he published a cartoon, now famous, in his newspaper. It showed a snake cut in several parts, each part labeled with the initials of one of the colonies. The caption read, JOIN, OR DIE.

At the convention, the delegates quickly agreed that the colonies ought to work out a plan for their common defense. A committee was put together to work out the details. Franklin was chosen to be on the committee. He presented his plan. The committee made some changes to it, but the result was based on

Franklin's idea. Known as the Albany Plan, it called for a president general to be appointed by the British government and a grand council to be elected by the colonies. This new government would deal with the Indians, govern the lands in the Northwest Territory, and raise taxes to support a colonial army.

In fact if this plan had gone through, it would have made a start on the United States that would be created some twenty years later. It was a very wise idea, for it would have given the Americans a great deal of say in their own government without them leaving the British Empire. Franklin later insisted that if it had been accepted, the American Revolution would never have been necessary. Given a voice in their government, the Americans might have happily remained part of the British Empire for many years thereafter.

But it never happened. The colonies were afraid that the plan would give too much power to the new joint government. The British government thought it would give too much power to the Americans. Franklin was right, and a great many others were wrong. It would not be the first time.

Chapter 3

THE SCIENTIST

B Y THE TIME HE WAS IN HIS LATE forties, Benjamin Franklin had accomplished a lot. He had made a success as a businessman, a writer, and a newspaper publisher. He had become important in the politics of Pennsylvania and was making his name known throughout the colonies. He had created the Pennsylvania militia, improved the American postal service, and worked out the Albany Plan. What was it about him that gave him such success?

This portrait of Franklin was made around the time he was concluding the peace treaty with England and France that finally ended the American Revolution. He was by now famous worldwide.

Undoubtedly, in part it was his ambition. He was determined to rise up, and he always looked around carefully to see what his next step ought to be. But there was something else. Benjamin Franklin was one of those people who forced himself to think carefully and clearly about whatever he undertook. He didn't just try something and hope that it would work out. Instead, he sat down and thought the whole thing over systematically, trying to figure out what would happen if he did one thing instead of another. He reasoned. He was rational.

As a result, he was often able to persuade people to accept his ideas. He would, in a newspaper article or a pamphlet, set forth his reasons for forming a militia, for creating a scheme for the common defense of the colonies or whatever else he thought of. Because he had thought the problem through carefully, his reasons usually made good sense. He always framed them in simple, direct language. In the end, people usually saw that Franklin was right.

We can also see another thing about his character. Benjamin Franklin was clearly public-spirited. He didn't have much to gain personally by working out a plan for joining the colonies or creating a militia. He simply saw that these would be for the good of everybody.

It was in his nature to act on his beliefs. Ben Franklin was, like many people, a mixture—interested in both his own success and what was good for everybody. As we shall see, there were many times when he sacrificed his own time and money to get what was best for his colony, his country, or the world at large.

By 1748 he had earned enough money to retire. He was now able to spend most of his time on public projects. He made an arrangement with another man to run his printing shop, with half the profits to go to Franklin. He would continue to edit the *Pennsylvania Gazette,*

Franklin in his lab. The large jar on the left of the table was a battery. The machine with the crank handle on the right was a device for creating an electric current. Early scientists did not understand electricity very well, and some were killed doing experiments. Franklin was knocked unconscious twice.

Poor Richard's Almanac, and other publications, for these were moneymakers and gave him great influence in the colonies. But he wanted to spend his time on things that interested him.

One of those things was electricity. In that day, electricity was a great mystery. Nobody knew what it was, what caused it, or what it could be used for, if anything. It had been known for centuries that if you rubbed amber with your hand it would attract lightweight objects like sheets of paper. (The word *electricity* comes from the Greek word for amber.) Later it was discovered that other materials, like sulfur, glass, and wax, would also attract things when rubbed. Nobody knew how this attraction worked. They assumed it was caused by some kind of fluid.

By the late 1600s some scientists were developing machines that could produce larger amounts of electricity. In such machines a globe or tube of amber, sulfur, or other substance would be rotated at high speed by a crank hand while the experimenter rubbed it with his hand. This electricity could be drawn off as sparks, or conducted somewhere by a wire or rod. It could also be fenced off by means of insulating material. Finally, in 1746, some scientists learned how to store electricity in primitive batteries.

At first these experimenters did not know what to do with this exciting "fluid," and they tended to play with it. One of them used to hang small boys upside down from the ceiling with insulated cords and draw sparks from their noses. Another experimenter put on a grand dinner party for his friends.

Although Franklin was quite serious about his experiments with electricity, he and others sometimes used them for entertainment. Here some of his friends play a game with electricity, although it is not clear what the point of it is. Note the dog at bottom right running in fear.

When they came into the dining room he charged the entire table with small amounts of electricity so that flames seemed to be dancing around the food, the silver candlesticks, the knives and forks. (Needless to say, these experimenters were using quite weak electric currents. The electric current found in houses today is much stronger and can hurt, or even kill, people who are unlucky enough to get touched by it. Students should *not* attempt experiments with household electricity.)

Ben Franklin was the type of person who always wanted to understand things. If he saw an interesting new device, he could not rest until he had examined it, figured out how it worked, and attempted to improve it. If he heard about an interesting sight, like a spectacular waterfall or a great river, he would want to see it for himself. Naturally when he heard about electricity he was eager to try some experiments.

In 1745 or 1746 Franklin got hold of a glass tube that could be spun to produce electricity. He soon had improved the first versions made in Philadelphia and gave some to friends also interested in the subject. Franklin wanted to show that Americans could make scientific experiments as well as Europeans.

He tried some experiments and quickly came up with what is one of the basic ideas in the science of electricity: an electric current flows from an object that has an excess of it to one that has a deficiency of it. He used the terms *positive* and *negative* to describe this idea, as we do today. Now we know that an electrical current is composed of electrons moving from one object to another. Actually it flows from negative to positive—the opposite of what Franklin thought. But Franklin had the basic idea right.

Scientists discovered that certain materials, when electrified, would repel, or force away, other materials. Here a ball hanging from a string is repelled by the larger electrified ball in the jar. When Franklin draws off the electricity from the larger ball with the rod he is holding, the small ball will swing toward it.

By the time Franklin retired, he was devoting much of his spare time to electrical experiments. He said, "I never was before engaged in any study that so totally engrossed my attention and my time as this has lately done." It was, in fact, a risky business. Franklin nearly killed himself twice with his experiments. After one accident he said, "I neither saw the flash, heard the report, nor felt the stroke. When my senses returned, I found myself on the floor." A few years later a scientist in Russia was killed during an electrical experiment.

Franklin was drawn to electricity out of his intensely curious nature, but he was also a very practical man, and he soon began looking for ways in which electricity could be of use to human beings. It occurred to Franklin, as it had to others, that electricity and lightning were much the same. Indeed, he speculated that perhaps lightning was electricity in a very powerful form.

Lightning was then a terrible and, to most people, mysterious force. It had been striking terror in humans for thousands of years by burning forests, killing animals and people, and smashing buildings. Churches were particularly likely to be hit, because their steeples were often the highest point in the area. In 1784 a German reported that in thirty-three years

386 steeples had been hit and 103 bell ringers had been killed in Germany. Barns, too, which often stood in open fields, were likely to be hit, destroying a farmer's crops and perhaps killing his livestock.

Others had noticed the resemblance between lightning and electricity, but Franklin gave the idea more thought. If a small electrical spark jumping from point to point produced a bright flash and a loud snap, "to what great distance may ten thousand acres of electrified cloud strike and give its fire, and how loud must be that crack?" he said. He knew that a metal point, like an arrowhead or the point of a knife, especially attracted electricity. Would lightning also be attracted by a point? "Let the experiment be made," he boldly pronounced.

Franklin concluded that lightning was electricity and worked out a plan for demonstrating this fact. But it was a French scientist who actually carried out the experiment by stationing a man in a little hut with a lightning rod set up nearby. A thunderstorm did come, but the man was unharmed. Later, Franklin performed his famous experiment with the key and the kite.

come up with the basic idea. Later Franklin too tried the famous kite and key experiment, simply to satisfy himself. But the Frenchman had already proven that he was right.

Franklin, however, did not rest there. He realized that the electricity building up in a storm could be drawn off via a rod or wire before it grew big enough to flash out as lightning. The electricity would, in effect, constantly "leak" away through the rod into the ground. Quickly Franklin devised his lightning rod—pointed rods, or wires, sticking a few feet above a building, with a wire attached leading into the ground, much as they are designed today. Lightning rods have saved tens of thousands of lives and countless millions of dollars in property.

The lightning rod was quickly recognized as a great blessing to humankind. Franklin was growing internationally famous. Poems were written about him and there were stories and articles in newspapers. He was elected to the Royal Society in England, got a special message of congratulations from the king of France, and was given an honorary degree from Harvard University, just outside Boston. The poor printer's apprentice from Boston had come a long way.

A satiric drawing shows French women wearing hats with "lightning rods" hanging from them. The fad for these hats was probably more imaginary than real, but the drawing shows the great stir the invention created in many countries.

Franklin could have made a fortune from his lightning rod if he had patented it, but he refused. He said he enjoyed the benefits from other people's inventions and was "glad of the opportunity to serve others. . . ." He did the same thing with another invention, a particular type of heating stove that was especially efficient. It was named the Franklin Stove.

Franklin's model of the stove he invented. It was designed so that the heated air circulated around the room. It was known as the Franklin Stove. Franklin did not patent it though, but rather allowed anyone to make it.

And there was much more. In 1727 Franklin had formed a club called the Junto. It was made up of men who got together to debate political issues. Like Franklin, they wanted to help improve the city of Philadelphia. He devoted much time and money to starting a library, which eventually became the first public library in Philadelphia. He helped reform the night watchmen of the city, who were spending more time in taverns than on duty. He put together a local fire brigade. (There were no city fire departments in those days.) He founded a philosophical society and an academy, which eventually became the University of Pennsylvania. He was everywhere, doing everything, much of it for the improvement of his city, the colony of Pennsylvania, America, and humanity in general. He liked doing these things. He had in his makeup the normal vanity—or perhaps a little more—that is in everybody, and he liked being admired for his good works. But it is also true that he had a genuine interest in accomplishing things, of seeing his projects grow and prosper.

It was, however, his electrical experiments, especially the lightning rod, that made him famous. And he would use that fame to play a major part in building the United States of America.

Chapter 4

TRIUMPH AND TRAGEDY

BY THE EARLY 1750S, WHILE FRANKLIN was working with electricity, the four-way squabbles between the French, English, American colonists, and Indians were heating up. What we now call the French and Indian War had started in 1753. The war was fought mainly in the Northwest Territory, Canada, and upstate New York. Although some of the Indians sided with the English and their American colonists, most were allied with the French or stayed out of the fighting altogether.

Franklin's portrait has been drawn hundreds of times. This one shows him in his later years reading a paper, a walking stick across his knees.

Many American militia regiments fought in this war, but the bulk of the fighting was done by professional British armies, with their well-trained soldiers and plentiful cannon. For several years the fighting went back and forth, with neither side able to get in a knockout blow.

To the British one big question was, who was going to pay for defending the colonies against the French and the Indians? The British thought that the Americans ought to contribute. Most Americans agreed, but they resented being told by the British how they were to be taxed. The Pennsylvanians especially disliked the taxing plan. The Pennsylvania Assembly argued heatedly against the plan, but the British would not give in. Finally the Assembly decided to send someone to London to argue directly with the authorities there. Ben Franklin was chosen.

He was thrilled. He had enjoyed his visit to England as a young man. Moreover, England was building a great empire, of which the American colonies were an important part. England was wealthy and possessed a mighty army and navy. It had great writers, painters, and musicians. London was a far more sophisticated and elegant place than Philadelphia. It was a larger stage with grander players. It would satisfy Benjamin Franklin's ambition to move into this larger world.

He left for London in June 1757. Being a man who could not stand to be idle, he passed the time away on the long ship journey by pulling together aphorisms from *Poor Richard's Almanac* to make a little book. It was published as *The Way to Wealth*, translated into many languages, and indeed was a way to wealth for Franklin.

He knew that he had a touch of vanity in his makeup, some pride in himself, and he assumed others did, too. He knew just what to say to such people and how to act around them. They in turn could see that Franklin was no rough farmer, but a very well-read man with good manners who could be counted on for witty conversation and stories of interesting things he had seen and heard. Franklin was also a good dinner companion. Sometimes he would go out to dinner five or six nights a week for weeks at a stretch. He said, "Being myself honored with visits from persons of quality and distinction, I was obliged for the credit of the province [Pennsylvania] to live in a fashion and expense suitable to the public character I sustain. . . ."

But Franklin was not simply swelling around London at dinners and teas. He was also writing a steady stream of letters and articles for English newspapers and magazines, giving Pennsylvania's side of the tax question. In sum, there were very few people in all the American colonies as well equipped for the job of convincing the British to change the tax plan as Franklin was.

Nevertheless the job would not be easy. The attitude of the British was that the colonies existed for British profits. Otherwise why bother with them?

The authorities were in no hurry to change the tax laws. Time dragged on. A year passed, then two and three. Franklin didn't mind—he liked London, and anyway, things in those days moved much slower. But finally he was able to get the British government to agree to a change in the law. Pennsylvania got a good deal of what it wanted, but not everything. Neither side had won, but at least Franklin had accomplished something.

In 1762 Franklin returned to Philadelphia. He was sorry to leave England, but it was time to go home. He had not seen his wife, Deborah, for five years.

But back home things were boiling. Tensions between England and the colonies were growing, mostly because of taxes. Within two years the Pennsylvania Assembly sent Franklin back to England. Soon both Georgia and Massachusetts also appointed Franklin as their representative in London. Franklin was becoming the chief voice for the American colonies in London.

The British government was still looking for ways to raise money in the colonies. In 1765 it put a tax on newspapers, cards, legal documents, almanacs, and other sorts of papers. The infamous Stamp Act incensed the colonists. There were riots. Many tax agents, fearful for their lives, resigned. It became clear that the Stamp Act could not be enforced without troops. Although nobody knew it yet, the march toward the American Revolution had begun.

Franklin, as was ever his way, tried to smooth things over. He believed that Americans ought to accept the Stamp Act in order to get the British government to give in on other points. But he soon realized that the American people would not accept it. Once again he began to pour out a stream of letters and articles for British newspapers explaining the American point of view.

Finally the British Parliament decided to have a hearing on the matter. Franklin was asked to testify. According to one witness he was like "a master examined by a panel of schoolboys. . . . He had the facts and figures at his fingertips. He oozed sweet reason, and he had a presence." When asked if Americans would submit to the Stamp Act if it were eased a little, he replied, "No, never, unless compelled by force of arms."

Meanwhile, back home, Americans were boycotting British goods. British makers of furniture, cloth, silverware, and much else, were losing a lot of money. Soon it was clear that the Stamp Act would cost more than it would bring in, and in March 1766 it was repealed. Franklin had not ended the Stamp Act by himself, the boycott was the key factor. But Franklin's clear arguments helped get the British to understand the colonists' point of view.

The Stamp Act was an important event in the crisis leading to the American Revolution. It put a tax on many items sold in America. The colonists in Boston and elsewhere rioted in protest. This is an artist's idea from a later time of a Stamp Act protest in Boston.

Chapter 5

WINNING THE REVOLUTION

FRANKLIN WOULD HAVE LIKED TO STAY on in England. Some people believe he intended to stay there for life. But by 1775 there were reasons for him to go home, and he did. Events were charging forward. Americans had been emboldened by their successful fight against the Stamp Act. In 1773 the British had changed the way tea was taxed, and once again Americans protested. The famous Boston Tea Party, where Americans dumped all the British tea from a ship into the harbor, was part of the protest.

By the 1770s Franklin's fame was spreading. This picture of him appeared in a German book in 1778.

The British now put in harsh laws against Massachusetts. Americans were ready to revolt. In April 1775 the British general there sent troops out of Boston to arrest some leaders of the revolt and capture guns and powder that had been stored in the village of Concord. The British met American volunteers called minutemen in the village of Lexington. A shot was fired—by whom, nobody knows—and the American Revolution was on.

Franklin arrived back in Philadelphia just as the Americans were gearing up to fight. George Washington was putting together an army, but he needed guns, uniforms, food for his troops, powder, and many other things. The brand-new United States was not a poor nation, but it had few factories for making war equipment. Much had to be bought in Europe. And where would the money come from? The new Congress tried to borrow money, and sometimes succeeded, but many lenders, both Americans and foreigners, were afraid that if the Americans lost their Revolution, they'd never get their money back.

Increasingly, Americans looked to France for help. France was a wealthy and powerful nation with its own colonies. The French were longtime rivals of the English and had lost Canada to them in the recent

This painting, by the famous illustrator Howard Pyle, shows the minutemen fighting the British on Lexington Green—the start of the revolution.

French and Indian War. Even though the Americans had fought against France in that war, the French would be glad to see America become free, because it would weaken their English rivals. Who knew, they might get Canada back, too. (They didn't, as it worked out.) Congress then decided to ask France for help. And the man they chose to do so was Benjamin Franklin.

Franklin would not be alone in France. Two other Americans were delegated to be there also. But Franklin, unquestionably, would be the key figure. He was seventy years old. He was not always in good health, but he accepted the challenge.

In October 1776 he left Philadelphia, taking with him two of his grandsons. Once again Deborah stayed home. In France he rented a very comfortable house in Passy, then a suburb of Paris. Paris was, if anything, even more elegant and refined than London. Franklin's job was to make friends with the rich and powerful Frenchmen who controlled things in France. The wives of such men often had great influence with them. Franklin, with his charm and wit, quickly made himself welcome at the homes of such women.

So it began all over again. There were endless dinners, concerts, plays, and happy hours with people who were becoming good friends. But there was plenty of hard work, too. Franklin had letters to write, petitions to get up, and articles to organize.

The job was not easy. Franklin had first to persuade the French that the Americans might actually beat the mighty British army and navy. He then had to get money from them—loans or, if possible, gifts. Once he got the money he would have to buy military supplies and see that they were shipped safely back to America.

But Franklin had one important thing going for him: he was famous in France, more famous than almost any Frenchman. He was practically worshipped by some French people. Medallions were made of him, poems written about him, many portraits painted. One artist said, "They strike him in silver, they mold him in china; one sees him now, at the last, well and faithfully rendered in medallions, in bracelets, on [candy] boxes, in medals, and on every mantelpiece worshipped no less than a household god." Franklin wrote to his daughter in Philadelphia that his face "was as well known as that of the moon."

Part of Franklin's great popularity was because of his electrical inventions. But Franklin also made a point of dressing and behaving in a very plain and down-to-earth style. This was in great contrast to the rich dress and elegant manners of French ladies and gentlemen.

In France Benjamin Franklin made a point of appearing to be a simple, plain, and honest man. His suit contrasts with the fancy dress worn by the French people around him in a gathering at the king's court.

France was far from a democratic nation, and the French people would rise in revolt only a few years later. Franklin's very democratic style appealed to ordinary French people. Bit by bit Franklin got supplies sent across the Atlantic.

But the big task was to bring the French into the American fight. The French needed assurance that the Americans could win. Washington had some small victories over the British in the battles of Trenton and Princeton, but mostly he was on the run. Then, in the summer of 1777, the Americans had a startling victory over the British at the Battle of Saratoga, where the British had to surrender a whole army. It was now clear that the Americans had a chance to win.

Franklin immediately sent word of the great American victory to the French king. At the same time, he asked for a formal treaty of friendship. The French had been stalling about this, for they knew that such a treaty would bring them into war against the English. They continued to stall.

The American victory at Saratoga had discouraged the British. They secretly sent representatives to Paris to meet with Franklin. They would give the Americans almost anything they wanted to end the war—except independence.

The Battle of Saratoga was one of the great victories for the Americans in the revolution. There came at a time when many people were concluding that the Americans could not win. Franklin was quick to use the victory to persuade the French that the Americans could win, but needed their help.

Franklin had no power to sign away American independence, but he did not tell the French this. Instead, he hinted that if the French did not come out openly on the American side, the Americans might make a deal with the British. The French did not want that, for it would leave the British stronger than ever. So they agreed to become allies to the Americans. Franklin's shrewd maneuvering had won them over.

It made all the difference. The French were slow to get moving, but by 1780 they had troops and ships in America.

By that time the British had conquered a good deal of the South. The French and American troops marched south. Outnumbered, the British general Cornwallis retreated into the little city of Yorktown, on a river near the sea. Cornwallis believed that the British navy would soon come sailing up the river and take his troops to safety.

Instead a French fleet sailed in. Caught between the French fleet on the water and the French and American troops on land, Cornwallis was in a desperate position. He held out for awhile, but in the end he was forced to surrender. When his troops marched out to hand over their weapons, a band played a tune called "The World Turned Upside Down." And indeed it had been. The ragtag American army had defeated the mighty British fighting machine with the help of the French.

Could the Americans have won without the French? Possibly. Many English people were growing very tired of the war, which was costing a lot of money and seemed to go on forever. But it would have been a much longer and harder struggle, and the Americans might have tired of it first. French help was critical.

Ben Franklin was not the only one responsible for getting the French to help. There were other factors.

The surrender of Lord Cornwallis at Yorktown is one of the most important events in American history. Although it would be more than two years before the peace treaty was signed, the American victory at Yorktown signaled that they had won.

But without Franklin's charm, fame, and cleverness, it might not have happened.

But there was more to come. The American victory at Yorktown ended the fighting, but there was still a peace treaty to be worked out. The British may have given up in America, but they had a powerful army and the mightiest navy in the world. Franklin was still in Paris and was in charge of negotiations for the Americans. He had now had many years of experience dealing with French and English governments, and he negotiated a deal that gave America full independence and settled other matters with the English. Once again he had performed a great service for his newly formed country.

This should have been enough of a life for one man: a success in business, author of works that are still read more than two hundred years later, important discoveries in science, great achievements as a statesman.

Yet there was one more task ahead of Franklin. The peace treaty with England was signed in 1783. Franklin lingered abroad until 1785 tying up loose ends and enjoying himself, then he finally returned to Philadelphia.

Meanwhile the new United States was facing a number of serious problems. These are too complicated to discuss in a short book. However, it seemed to many wise men, including George Washington, James Madison, and Alexander Hamilton, that the American government needed to be thoroughly revised to make it stronger. A meeting of delegates from the states was called in Philadelphia for the spring of 1787. This would be the great Constitutional Convention at which the famous United States Constitution, so important to Americans, was written.

Many great men were there including, of course, Benjamin Franklin, although he was now over eighty years old and in poor health. Nonetheless, he went to the meetings almost every day through that summer.

He said little but listened carefully. The simple fact that he was there mattered. If he had stayed away, many people would have decided that Ben Franklin opposed the constitution and would have opposed it themselves.

Finally, on September 15, the remarkable document was finished. There were several people at the convention who opposed it. One man said that it would produce a "monarchy or tyrannical aristocracy."

Many pictures have been painted of the signing of the U.S. Constitution. Actually, nobody was in the room except the members of the convention, so we cannot be completely sure what the event looked like. This is as good a guess as any.

Ben Franklin decided to speak out. Too ill to speak himself, he asked another man to read his message. It said:

> *Mr. President, I confess that there are several parts of this Constitution of which I do not approve, but I am not sure that I shall never approve them. . . . For having lived long I have experienced many instances of being obliged . . . to change opinions on even important subjects. . . . It therefore astonishes me, sir, to find this system approaching so near to perfection as it does. . . . Thus I consent, sir, to this Constitution, because I expect no better, and because I am not sure that it is not the best.*

Franklin was once again right. The United States Constitution is today one of the most admired documents ever written by anyone anywhere. His word alone did not, of course, persuade the delegates to sign it. Most of them were going to sign anyway. But in the United States, what Ben Franklin thought mattered. And it mattered because he had so often taken the trouble to think things through carefully and had more often than not made the right decision.

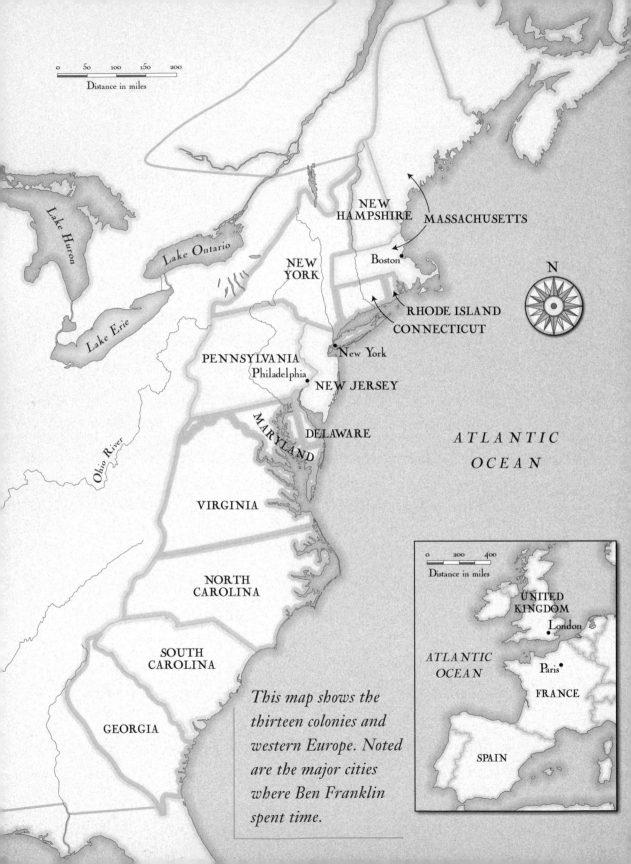

Distance in miles
0 50 100 150 200

Lake Huron

Lake Ontario

Lake Erie

NEW
HAMPSHIRE   MASSACHUSETTS

NEW
YORK   Boston

RHODE ISLAND
CONNECTICUT

N

Ohio River

PENNSYLVANIA   New York
Philadelphia   NEW JERSEY

MARYLAND   DELAWARE

ATLANTIC
OCEAN

VIRGINIA

NORTH
CAROLINA

Distance in miles
0 200 400

SOUTH
CAROLINA

UNITED
KINGDOM
London

ATLANTIC
OCEAN

GEORGIA

*This map shows the
thirteen colonies and
western Europe. Noted
are the major cities
where Ben Franklin
spent time.*

Paris
FRANCE

SPAIN

Author's Note on Sources

Anyone interested in Benjamin Franklin should read his famous autobiography, which advanced students will be able to do. There are several editions currently available. Two inexpensive ones are *Benjamin Franklin: The Autobiography* (Vintage Library: New York, 1990) and *Benjamin Franklin: The Autobiography and Other Writings* (Penguin: New York, 1986). There are two recent excellent scholarly biographies: *The First American*, by H.W. Brands (Anchor: New York, 2000) and *Benjamin Franklin*, by Edmund S. Morgan (Yale: New Haven, 2002).

For students there is *Benjamin Franklin*, by Victoria Sherrow (Lerner: Minneapolis, 2002).

INDEX

James Lincoln Collier has written many books, both fiction and nonfiction, for children and adults. His interests span history, biography, and historical fiction. He is an authority on the history of jazz and performs weekly on the trombone in New York City.

My Brother Sam Is Dead was named a Newbery Honor Book and a Jane Addams Honor Book and was a finalist for a National Book Award. *Jump Ship to Freedom* and *War Comes to Willy Freemen* were each named a notable Children's Trade Book in the Field of Social Studies by the National Council for Social Studies and the Children's Book Council. Collier received the Christopher Award for *Decision in Philadelphia: The Constitutional Convention of 1787*. He lives in Pawling, New York.